CKR

Under the Sea

Puffer Fish

by Jody Sullivan Rake

Consulting Editor: Gail Saunders-Smith, PhD

Consultant: Debbie Nuzzolo
Education Manager
SeaWorld, San Diego, California

Mankato, Minnesota

Pebble Plus is published by Capstone Press,
151 Good Counsel Drive, P.O. Box 669, Mankato, Minnesota 56002.
www.capstonepress.com

1 2 3 4 5 6 11 10 09 08 07 06

Library of Congress Cataloging-in-Publication Data
Rake, Jody Sullivan.
    Puffer fish / by Jody Sullivan Rake.
    p. cm.—(Pebble Plus. Under the sea)
    Summary: "Simple text and photographs describe the lives of puffer fish"—Provided by publisher.
    Includes bibliographical references and index.
    ISBN-13: 978-0-7368-6364-3 (hardcover)
    ISBN-10: 0-7368-6364-8 (hardcover)
1. Puffers (Fish) I. Title. II. Series: Under the sea (Mankato, Minn.)
QL638.T32R35 2007
597'.64—dc22   2005036009

Editorial Credits
Mari Schuh, editor; Juliette Peters, set designer; Patrick D. Dentinger, book designer; Kelly Garvin,
    photo researcher/photo editor

Photo Credits
Corbis/Stephen Frink, 11; Tom Brakefield, 5
Corel, 1
Jeff Rotman, 9
Minden Pictures/Fred Bavendam, 7
Nature Picture Library/Florian Graner, 12–13; Georgette Douwma, 16–17, 19, 21
PhotoDisc Inc., back cover
Seapics/Franco Banfi, 15
Tom Stack & Associates Inc./Tom Stack, cover

Note to Parents and Teachers

The Under the Sea set supports national science standards related to the diversity and
unity of life. This book describes and illustrates puffer fish. The images support early
readers in understanding the text. The repetition of words and phrases helps early
readers learn new words. This book also introduces early readers to subject-specific
vocabulary words, which are defined in the Glossary section. Early readers may need
assistance to read some words and to use the Table of Contents, Glossary, Read More,
Internet Sites, and Index sections of the book.

Table of Contents

What Are Puffer Fish?

Puffer fish are plump fish.

Spots and stripes
cover some puffer fish.

Puffer fish gulp water
to puff up like a balloon.
Then they are too big
for predators to eat.

Thick skin covers puffer fish.

The skin stretches

when they puff up.

9

Some puffer fish are
as big as a football.
Other puffer fish are
about the size of a banana.

Body Parts

Puffer fish have fins.

They wave their fins to swim.

Puffer fish teeth
look like a beak.

The teeth are joined together.

What Puffer Fish Do

Puffer fish eat hard food.
Their strong teeth crush
corals, sea urchins,
and shellfish.

Some puffer fish
body parts are poisonous.
Predators that eat
puffer fish can die.

Under the Sea

Puffer fish swim

in warm water

under the sea.

Glossary

beak—the hard mouth parts that some animals have instead of teeth; puffer fish teeth are joined to form a beak.

fin—a flexible body part that helps an ocean animal swim; puffer fish have five fins.

plump—full and round

poisonous—having a substance that can harm or kill an animal or a person

predator—an animal that hunts and eats other animals

shellfish—an ocean animal kept safe by a shell; clams, oysters, and crabs are shellfish.

Read More

Garrett, Ann, and Gene-Michael Higney. *Fins and Flippers, Scales and Nippers.* New York: Mondo, 2003.

Knox, Barbara. *ABC Under the Sea: An Ocean Life Alphabet Book.* Alphabet Books. Mankato, Minn.: A+ Books, 2003.

Walsh, Melanie. *Ocean Animals.* Tiny Teethers. Cambridge, Mass.: Candlewick Press, 2002.

Internet Sites

FactHound offers a safe, fun way to find Internet sites related to this book. All of the sites on FactHound have been researched by our staff.

Here's how:

1. Visit *www.facthound.com*

2. Choose your grade level.

3. Type in this book ID **0736863648** for age-appropriate sites. You may also browse subjects by clicking on letters, or by clicking on pictures and words.

4. Click on the **Fetch It** button.

FactHound will fetch the best sites for you!

Index

Word Count: 121
Grade: 1
Early-Intervention Level: 13